Great Works Instructional Guides for Literature

Esperanza Rising

A guide for the book by Pam Muñoz Ryan
Great Works Author: Kristin Kemp, M.A.Ed.

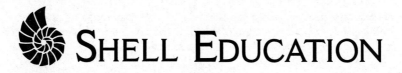

SHELL EDUCATION

Publishing Credits

Corinne Burton, M.A.Ed., *President*; Emily R. Smith, M.A.Ed., *Content Director*; Lee Aucoin, *Multimedia Designer*; Jill K. Mulhall, M.Ed., *Editor*; Stephanie Bernard, *Assistant Editor*; Don Tran, *Graphic Designer*

Image Credits

iStock (cover)

Standards

© 2007 Teachers of English to Speakers of Other Languages, Inc. (TESOL)
© 2007 Board of Regents of the University of Wisconsin System. World-Class Instructional Design and Assessment (WIDA)
© Copyright 2010. National Governors Association Center for Best Practices and Council of Chief State School Officers. All rights reserved.

Shell Education

a division of Teacher Created Materials
5301 Oceanus Drive
Huntington Beach, CA 92649-1030
ISBN 978-1-4807-8512-0
https://www.tcmpub.com/shell-education
© 2017 Shell Educational Publishing, Inc.

Table of Contents

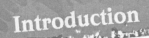

How to Use This Literature Guide

Today's standards demand rigor and relevance in the reading of complex texts. The units in this series guide teachers in a rich and deep exploration of worthwhile works of literature for classroom study. The most rigorous instruction can also be interesting and engaging!

Many current strategies for effective literacy instruction have been incorporated into these instructional guides for literature. Throughout the units, text-dependent questions are used to determine comprehension of the book as well as student interpretation of the vocabulary words. The books chosen for the series are complex exemplars of carefully crafted works of literature. Close reading is used throughout the units to guide students toward revisiting the text and using textual evidence to respond to prompts orally and in writing. Students must analyze the story elements in multiple assignments for each section of the book. All of these strategies work together to rigorously guide students through their study of literature.

The next few pages will make clear how to use this guide for a purposeful and meaningful literature study. Each section of this guide is set up in the same way to make it easier for you to implement the instruction in your classroom.

Theme Thoughts

The great works of literature used throughout this series have important themes that have been relevant to people for many years. Many of the themes will be discussed during the various sections of this instructional guide. However, it would also benefit students to have independent time to think about the key themes of the novel.

Before students begin reading, have them complete *Pre-Reading Theme Thoughts* (page 13). This graphic organizer will allow students to think about the themes outside the context of the story. They'll have the opportunity to evaluate statements based on important themes and defend their opinions. Be sure to have students keep their papers for comparison to the *Post-Reading Theme Thoughts* (page 64). This graphic organizer is similar to the pre-reading activity. However, this time, students will be answering the questions from the point of view of one of the characters in the novel. They have to think about how the character would feel about each statement and defend their thoughts. To conclude the activity, have students compare what they thought about the themes before they read the novel to what the characters discovered during the story.

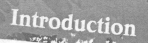

How to Use This Literature Guide *(cont.)*

Vocabulary

Each teacher overview page has definitions and sentences about how key vocabulary words are used in the section. These words should be introduced and discussed with students. There are two student vocabulary activity pages in each section. On the first page, students are asked to define the ten words chosen by the author of this unit. On the second page in most sections, each student will select at least eight words that he or she finds interesting or difficult. For each section, choose one of these pages for your students to complete. With either assignment, you may want to have students get into pairs to discuss the meanings of the words. Allow students to use reference guides to define the words. Monitor students to make sure the definitions they have found are accurate and relate to how the words are used in the text.

On some of the vocabulary student pages, students are asked to answer text-related questions about the vocabulary words. The following question stems will help you create your own vocabulary questions if you'd like to extend the discussion.

- How does this word describe _____'s character?
- In what ways does this word relate to the problem in this story?
- How does this word help you understand the setting?
- In what ways is this word related to the story's solution?
- Describe how this word supports the novel's theme of . . . .
- What visual images does this word bring to your mind?
- For what reasons might the author have chosen to use this particular word?

At times, more work with the words will help students understand their meanings. The following quick vocabulary activities are a good way to further study the words.

- Have students practice their vocabulary and writing skills by creating sentences and/or paragraphs in which multiple vocabulary words are used correctly and with evidence of understanding.
- Students can play vocabulary concentration. Students make a set of cards with the words and a separate set of cards with the definitions. Then, students lay the cards out on the table and play concentration. The goal of the game is to match vocabulary words with their definitions.
- Students can create word journal entries about the words. Students choose words they think are important and then describe why they think each word is important within the novel.

How to Use This Literature Guide (cont.)

Analyzing the Literature

After students have read each section, hold small-group or whole-class discussions. Questions are written at two levels of complexity to allow you to decide which questions best meet the needs of your students. The Level 1 questions are typically less abstract than the Level 2 questions. Level 1 is indicated by a square, while Level 2 is indicated by a triangle. These questions focus on the various story elements, such as character, setting, and plot. Student pages are provided if you want to assign these questions for individual student work before your group discussion. Be sure to add further questions as your students discuss what they've read. For each question, a few key points are provided for your reference as you discuss the novel with students.

Reader Response

In today's classrooms, there are often great readers who are below-average writers. So much time and energy is spent in classrooms getting students to read on grade level that little time is left to focus on writing skills. To help teachers include more writing in their daily literacy instruction, each section of this guide has a literature-based reader response prompt. Each of the three genres of writing is used in the reader responses within this guide: narrative, informative/explanatory, and opinion/argument. Students have a choice between two prompts for each reader response. One response requires students to make connections between the reading and their own lives. The other prompt requires students to determine text-to-text connections or connections within the text.

Close Reading the Literature

Within each section, students are asked to closely reread a short section of text. Since some versions of the novels have different page numbers, the selections are described by chapter and location, along with quotations to guide the readers. After each close reading, there are text-dependent questions to be answered by students.

Encourage students to read each question one at a time and then go back to the text and discover the answer. Work with students to ensure that they use the text to determine their answers rather than making unsupported inferences. Once students have answered the questions, discuss what they discovered. Suggested answers are provided in the answer key.

How to Use This Literature Guide (cont.)

Close Reading the Literature (cont.)

The generic, open-ended stems below can be used to write your own text-dependent questions if you would like to give students more practice.

- Give evidence from the text to support . . . .
- Justify your thinking using text evidence about . . . .
- Find evidence to support your conclusions about . . . .
- What text evidence helps the reader understand . . . ?
- Use the book to tell why _____ happens.
- Based on events in the story, ...
- Use text evidence to describe why . . . .

Making Connections

The activities in this section help students make cross-curricular connections to writing, mathematics, science, social studies, or the fine arts. Each of these types of activities requires higher-order thinking skills from students.

Creating with the Story Elements

It is important to spend time discussing the common story elements in literature. Understanding the characters, setting, and plot can increase students' comprehension and appreciation of the story. If teachers discuss these elements daily, students will more likely internalize the concepts and look for the elements in their independent reading. Another important reason for focusing on the story elements is that students will be better writers if they think about how the stories they read are constructed.

Students are given three options for working with the story elements. They are asked to create something related to the characters, setting, or plot of the novel. Students are given a choice in this activity so that they can decide to complete the activity that most appeals to them. Different multiple intelligences are used so that the activities are diverse and interesting to all students.

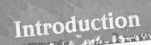

How to Use This Literature Guide (cont.)

Culminating Activity

This open-ended, cross-curricular activity requires higher-order thinking and allows for a creative product. Students will enjoy getting the chance to share what they have discovered through reading the novel. Be sure to allow them enough time to complete the activity at school or home.

Comprehension Assessment

The questions in this section are modeled after current standardized tests to help students analyze what they've read and prepare for tests they may see in their classrooms. The questions are dependent on the text and require critical-thinking skills to answer.

Response to Literature

The final post-reading activity is an essay based on the text that also requires further research by students. This is a great way to extend this book into other curricular areas. A suggested rubric is provided for teacher reference.

Correlation to the Standards

Shell Education is committed to producing educational materials that are research and standards based. As part of this effort, we have correlated all of our products to the academic standards of all 50 states, the District of Columbia, the Department of Defense Dependents Schools, and all Canadian provinces.

Purpose and Intent of Standards

The Every Student Succeeds Act (ESSA) mandates that all states adopt challenging academic standards that help students meet the goal of college and career readiness. While many states already adopted academic standards prior to ESSA, the act continues to hold states accountable for detailed and comprehensive standards. Standards are statements that describe the criteria necessary for students to meet specific academic goals. They define the knowledge, skills, and content students should acquire at each level. State standards are used in the development of our products, so educators can be assured they meet state academic requirements.

How to Find Standards Correlations

To print a customized correlation report of this product for your state, visit our website at **www.teachercreatedmaterials.com/administrators/correlations/** and follow the online directions. If you require assistance in printing correlation reports, please contact our Customer Service Department at 1-877-777-3450.

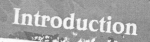

Correlation to the Standards (cont.)

Standards Correlation Chart

The lessons in this guide were written to support today's college and career readiness standards. This chart indicates which sections of this guide address which standards.

College and Career Readiness Standards	Section
Read closely to determine what the text says explicitly and to make logical inferences from it; cite specific textual evidence when writing or speaking to support conclusions drawn from the text.	Analyzing the Literature Sections 1–5; Close Reading the Literature Sections 1–5; Making Connections Section 1; Post-Reading Response to Literature
Determine central ideas or themes of a text and analyze their development; summarize the key supporting details and ideas.	Analyzing the Literature Sections 1–5; Reader Response Sections 1–5; Making Connections Sections 2,4; Creating with the Story Elements Sections 1–2; Post-Reading Response to Literature
Analyze how and why individuals, events, or ideas develop and interact over the course of a text.	Analyzing the Literature Sections 1–5; Creating with the Story Elements Sections 1–5
Interpret words and phrases as they are used in a text, including determining technical, connotative, and figurative meanings, and analyze how specific word choices shape meaning or tone.	Vocabulary Sections 1–5
Read and comprehend complex literary and informational texts independently and proficiently.	Entire Unit
Write arguments to support claims in an analysis of substantive topics or texts using valid reasoning and relevant and sufficient evidence.	Analyzing the Literature Sections 1–5; Close Reading the Literature Sections 1–5; Reader Response Sections 2–3, 5
Write informative/explanatory texts to examine and convey complex ideas and information clearly and accurately through the effective selection, organization, and analysis of content.	Reader Response Sections 1–2, 4; Making Connections Section 5; Post-Reading Response to Literature
Write narratives to develop real or imagined experiences or events using effective technique, well-chosen details and well-structured event sequences.	Reader Response Sections 1, 3–5; Creating with the Story Elements Sections 2, 4
Produce clear and coherent writing in which the development, organization, and style are appropriate to task, purpose, and audience.	Reader Response Sections 1–5; Post-Reading Response to Literature
Conduct short as well as more sustained research projects based on focused questions, demonstrating understanding of the subject under investigation.	Analyzing the Literature Sections 1–5; Reader Response Sections 1–5
Draw evidence from literary or informational texts to support analysis, reflection, and research.	Post-Reading Response to Literature

Correlation to the Standards (cont.)

Standards Correlation Chart (cont.)

College and Career Readiness Standards	Section
Write routinely over extended time frames (time for research, reflection, and revision) and shorter time frames (a single sitting or a day or two) for a range of tasks, purposes, and audiences.	Reader Response Sections 1–5; Post-Reading Response to Literature
Evaluate a speaker's point of view, reasoning, and use of evidence and rhetoric.	Culminating Activity
Present information, findings, and supporting evidence such that listeners can follow the line of reasoning and the organization, development, and style are appropriate to task, purpose, and audience.	Culminating Activity
Adapt speech to a variety of contexts and communicative tasks, demonstrating command of formal English when indicated or appropriate.	Culminating Activity
Demonstrate command of the conventions of standard English grammar and usage when writing or speaking.	Entire Unit
Demonstrate command of the conventions of standard English capitalization, punctuation, and spelling when writing.	Entire Unit
Apply knowledge of language to understand how language functions in different contexts, to make effective choices for meaning or style, and to comprehend more fully when reading or listening.	Reader Response Sections 1–5; Post-Reading Response to Literature
Determine or clarify the meaning of unknown and multiple-meaning words and phrases by using context clues, analyzing meaningful word parts, and consulting general and specialized reference materials, as appropriate.	Vocabulary Sections 1–5
Demonstrate understanding of figurative language, word relationships, and nuances in word meanings.	Making Connections Section 5
Acquire and use accurately a range of general academic and domain-specific words and phrases sufficient for reading, writing, speaking, and listening at the college and career readiness level; demonstrate independence in gathering vocabulary knowledge when encountering an unknown term important to comprehension or expression.	Vocabulary Sections 1–5

TESOL and WIDA Standards

The lessons in this book promote English language development for English language learners. The following TESOL and WIDA English Language Development Standards are addressed through the activities in this book:

- Standard 1: English language learners communicate for social and instructional purposes within the school setting.

- Standard 2: English language learners communicate information, ideas and concepts necessary for academic success in the content area of language arts.

About the Author—Pam Muñoz Ryan

Though a voracious reader and storyteller in her childhood, Pam Muñoz Ryan did not even think about becoming an author until adulthood. Growing up in Bakersfield, California, she spent a lot of time with her family, especially her grandmother. Every day after school, Ryan would walk to her grandmother's house and stay there until her parents got home from work.

Before fifth grade, Ryan moved to the other side of town, which meant she had to attend a new school, and she no longer lived within walking distance of her grandmother. She turned to the nearby library and its books to fill her time. In junior high, she was the editor of the school newspaper, and in high school, she excelled in reading and writing. She knew she wanted a career in literature and decided to become a teacher.

After graduating from San Diego State University, Ryan became a bilingual teacher for Head Start. When she and her husband had children, she decided to quit teaching and stay home. When her children were a bit older, she went back to San Diego State University to pursue her master's degree. It was there that a professor asked her if she had ever considered writing. Within weeks, a colleague also asked Ryan if she would help her write a book. These two events planted a seed in Ryan's mind, and she decided to follow this new dream.

Ryan has written more than 40 books and has received many awards including the National Education Association's Civil and Human Rights Award, the Virginia Hamilton Literary Award for Multicultural Literature, and two Willa Cather Awards. *Esperanza Rising* is one of her most popular and acclaimed works. It is based on the life of Ryan's grandmother, who was also named Esperanza. Like the character in the novel, the real Esperanza grew up very wealthy and lived on a large ranch. After her father's death, she and her family left for the United States, enduring many of the same hardships and joys as the fictional Esperanza.

Ryan lives near San Diego in North County, California, with her husband. She enjoys going to the beach, traveling, reading, and spending time with her four grown children and their families.

Possible Texts for Text Comparisons

Other books authored by Pam Muñoz Ryan could be used as enriching text comparisons. Titles include *Becoming Naomi León*, *Paint the Wind*, and *Riding Freedom*. These books have strong female lead characters and have themes of self-discovery.

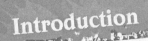

Book Summary of *Esperanza Rising*

Twelve-year-old Esperanza Ortega leads an idyllic life in 1930s Mexico. Her father owns a large and profitable ranch, her family adores her, and she is surrounded by beautiful dresses and dolls. On the eve of her thirteenth birthday, however, everything changes when bandits kill Esperanza's papa. According to Mexican law, Mama can own the house but not the land; it passes on to Papa's cruel stepbrother, who wants to marry Mama. When she refuses, he burns down the house and threatens more reprisals. Mama and Esperanza escape in the night, leaving behind Esperanza's injured grandmother, Abuelita.

Esperanza and her mother travel to the United States with Alfonso, Papa's friend and boss of the field workers, and his family. Settling at a work camp in the San Joaquin Valley of California, Mama finds a job in the fields, and Esperanza works at the camp. For the first time, Esperanza must do laundry, sweep, and care for children. It is a hard life for her, made even harder when Mama becomes very ill with Valley Fever and must go to the hospital for several months.

Now responsible for making money for her family, Esperanza joins the workers in the fields. She pays for Mama's hospital bills and saves the rest to bring Abuelita back to them. Over time, Esperanza begins to change. Her strong work ethic gets her rehired for each crop's harvest. She renews her friendship with Miguel, Alfonso's son, whom she has known since birth. She even makes new friends—Miguel's young cousin, Isabel, and Marta, an angry young woman who is always trying to organize the workers to strike.

At last, Mama is well enough to come home. Shortly after, Esperanza and Miguel have a horrible fight, and he is gone the next morning with all of the money she had been saving. She is furious at first, but he returns days later with Abuelita. Overcome with joy at being surrounded by family and friends, Esperanza realizes she has everything she needs.

Cross-Curricular Connection

This book could be used in a social studies unit on immigration or the Dust Bowl, a science unit on growing fruits and vegetables, or a unit on the Spanish language and Mexican culture.

Possible Texts for Text Sets

- Hengel, Katherine. 2014. *Garden to Table: A Kid's Guide to Planting, Growing, and Preparing Food*. Minneapolis: Mighty Media Junior Readers.

- Hesse, Karen. 2009. *Out of the Dust*. Wilmington: Great Source.

- Jiménez, Francisco. 1997. *The Circuit: Stories from the Life of a Migrant Child*. Albuquerque: University of New Mexico Press.

- Perez, Amada Irma. 2009. *My Diary from Here to There*. New York: Lee and Low Books, Inc.

Name _____

Date _____

Pre-Reading Theme Thoughts

Directions: Read each of the statements in the first column. Decide if you agree or disagree with the statements. Record your opinion by marking an X in Agree or Disagree for each statement. Explain your choices in the fourth column. There are no right or wrong answers.

Statement	Agree	Disagree	Explain Your Answer
If something is unfair, people should fight for change.			
Poor people and rich people should not be friends.			
Going through a hard experience makes a person stronger.			
Starting over is too hard and not worth it.			

Teacher Plans

Vocabulary Overview

Ten key words from this section are provided below with definitions and sentences about how the words are used in the book. Choose one of the vocabulary activity sheets (pages 15 or 16) for students to complete as they read this section. Monitor students as they work to ensure the definitions they have found are accurate and relate to the text. Finally, discuss these important vocabulary words with students. If you think these words or other words in the section warrant more time devoted to them, there are suggestions in the introduction for other vocabulary activities (page 5).

Word	Definition	Sentence about Text
premonition (ch. 1)	a feeling that something is going to happen, especially something bad	When she pricks her thumb, Esperanza has a **premonition** of bad luck.
capricious (ch. 1)	changing suddenly in mood or behavior	Esperanza loves free-spirited Abuelita for her **capricious** ways.
propriety (ch. 1)	having correct and proper behavior	Abuelita looks very distinguished and is known for her great **propriety**.
resurrected (ch. 1)	brought back to life	Papa and Alfonso work to **resurrect** the ranch's neglected rose garden.
indignation (ch. 2)	anger caused by something wrong or unfair	Mama and Abuelita feel **indignation** when Tío Luis wears Papa's belt buckle.
pretentious (ch. 2)	acting wealthier or more important than one really is	Tío Luis can build a bigger, more **pretentious** house anywhere on the land.
pervaded (ch. 2)	spread through all the parts of something	The scent of the sweet, overripe papayas **pervades** the air.
visa (ch. 3)	papers showing a person can enter, leave, or stay in a country	Mama knows they cannot enter the United States without a **visa**.
discreetly (ch. 3)	to do something carefully in order to avoid being noticed	Abuelita's sisters can **discreetly** get duplicates of the visas.
valise (ch. 3)	a small bag or suitcase used for traveling	Esperanza fills her **valise** with clothes, tamales, and the doll from Papa.

Name _____

Date _____

Understanding Vocabulary Words

Directions: The following words appear in this section of the book. Use context clues and reference materials to determine an accurate definition for each word.

Word	Definition
premonition (ch. 1)	
capricious (ch. 1)	
propriety (ch. 1)	
resurrected (ch. 1)	
indignation (ch. 2)	
pretentious (ch. 2)	
pervaded (ch. 2)	
visa (ch. 3)	
discreetly (ch. 3)	
valise (ch. 3)	

Name _____

Date _____

During-Reading Vocabulary Activity

Directions: As you read these chapters, record at least eight important words on the lines below. Try to find interesting, difficult, intriguing, special, or funny words. Your words can be long or short. They can be hard or easy to spell. After each word, use context clues in the text and reference materials to define the word.

- _____

- _____

- _____

- _____

- _____

- _____

- _____

- _____

- _____

Directions: Respond to these questions about the words in this section.

1. What example is given to illustrate Abuelita's **capricious** behavior?

   _____

   _____

2. Why must Abuelita's sisters replace the visas **discreetly**?

   _____

   _____

Analyzing the Literature

Provided below are discussion questions you can use in small groups, with the whole class, or for written assignments. Each question is given at two levels so you can choose the right question for each group of students. Activity sheets with these questions are provided (pages 18–19) if you want students to write their responses. For each question, a few key discussion points are provided for your reference.

Story Element	■ Level 1	▲ Level 2	Key Discussion Points
Setting	Why are Esperanza and Mama worried about bandits when Papa is out on the land?	How is the post-Mexican Revolution setting important for the story?	The story is set in 1930, 10 years after the revolution. Many poor Mexicans are still angry with large landowners like Papa. These groups of "bandits" travel around, looking to rob and even kill any wealthy ranchers they find.
Character	Compare Esperanza and Miguel's relationship from childhood to now.	Why does Esperanza and Miguel's relationship change from when they were younger?	As children, Esperanza and Miguel were very close and played together. When they are older, they barely talk and Miguel addresses her as "my queen." Their relationship changes when Esperanza realizes she is a wealthy rancher's daughter, and Miguel is a servant. She tells him they stand on different sides of a deep river.
Plot	What do Mama and Esperanza learn about Papa's will?	Why does Papa's will prompt Tío Luis to propose marriage to Mama?	Papa's will leaves the house and vineyard to Mama. But it leaves the land to the banker, Tío Luis, because women do not customarily own land. Tío Luis proposes to Mama so he can have it all, including the respect and reputation of Mama. He wants to enter politics and feels being married to her will help his career.
Plot	Why are Alfonso and his family moving to the United States?	Why does Alfonso feel that moving to the United States will be better than staying in Mexico?	Alfonso has family in the United States that can help them find housing and jobs. He knows he and his family will always be servants in Mexico, no matter how hard they work. Tío Luis will not treat them with any kindness or respect, so Alfonso will not stay at the ranch to work for him.

Name _____

Date _____

■ Analyzing the Literature

Directions: Think about the section you just read. Read each question and state your response with textual evidence.

1. Why are Esperanza and Mama worried about bandits when Papa is out on the land?

   _____

   _____

   _____

   _____

2. Compare Esperanza and Miguel's relationship from childhood to now.

   _____

   _____

   _____

   _____

3. What do Mama and Esperanza learn about Papa's will?

   _____

   _____

   _____

   _____

4. Why are Alfonso and his family moving to the United States?

   _____

   _____

   _____

   _____

Name _____

Date _____

▲ Analyzing the Literature

Directions: Think about the section you just read. Read each question and state your response with textual evidence.

1. How is the post-Mexican Revolution setting important for the story?

_____

_____

_____

_____

2. Why does Esperanza and Miguel's relationship change from when they were younger?

_____

_____

_____

_____

3. Why does Papa's will prompt Tío Luis to propose marriage to Mama?

_____

_____

_____

_____

4. Why does Alfonso feel that moving to the United States will be better than staying in Mexico?

_____

_____

_____

_____

Name _____

Date _____

Reader Response

Directions: Choose one of the following prompts about this section to answer. Be sure you include a topic sentence in your response, use textual evidence to support your opinion, and provide a strong conclusion that summarizes your opinion.

Writing Prompts

- **Narrative Piece**—Esperanza is very excited about her birthday traditions—the party, the serenade, and the gifts. What traditions do you have in your family that you look forward to?

- **Informative/Explanatory Piece**—Esperanza and Miguel both say that in Mexico, they stand on different sides of a river. What does this mean? Do you think it will be different in the United States?

_____

_____

_____

_____

_____

_____

_____

_____

_____

_____

_____

_____

_____

Name _____

Date _____

Close Reading the Literature

Directions: Closely reread the section in chapter 3 when Mama explains her idea in Alfonso's home. Begin with, "They all crowded into Hortensia and Alfonso's tiny bedroom," and stop with, "And for the first time since Papa died, everyone laughed." Read each question and then revisit the text to find evidence that supports your answer.

1. According to Alfonso, why would it be difficult for Mama and Esperanza to stay in Mexico?

   _____

   _____

   _____

2. Why must Mama's plan be kept a secret? Use the text to support your answer.

   _____

   _____

   _____

3. Explain the purpose of the sentence, "Do not be afraid to start over." Use Abuelita's story from her childhood in your answer.

   _____

   _____

   _____

4. Use details from the text to describe Esperanza's thoughts about moving.

   _____

   _____

   _____

Name _____

Date _____

Making Connections–Superstitions

Directions: A superstition is something people believe even though there is no logical reason and it may not make sense. An example is thinking it is bad luck to open an umbrella indoors. Think of superstitions, and fill in each column. Then, answer the questions below.

Bad luck	Good luck
• _____ _____	• _____ _____
• _____ _____	• _____ _____
• _____ _____	• _____ _____

1. What bad luck superstition happens to Esperanza in the book?

   _____

   _____

2. Why do you think people believe in superstitions?

   _____

   _____

3. Do you believe in any superstitions? Why or why not?

   _____

   _____

Name _____

Date _____

Creating with the Story Elements

Directions: Thinking about the story elements of character, setting, and plot in a novel is very important to understanding what is happening and why. Complete **one** of the following activities based on what you've read so far. Be creative and have fun!

Characters

Create a character web for Esperanza, Mama, or Abuelita. List at least three traits for the character you choose and give an example from the book to support each trait.

Setting

Draw a map of El Rancho de las Rosas. Include Esperanza's house, the servants' quarters, the rose garden, the vineyard, and the fields.

Plot

Make a flow chart with at least five important events that have happened so far in the story. For each event, include a quotation from the text to describe it.

Vocabulary Overview

Ten key words from this section are provided below with definitions and sentences about how the words are used in the book. Choose one of the vocabulary activity sheets (pages 25 or 26) for students to complete as they read this section. Monitor students as they work to ensure the definitions they have found are accurate and relate to the text. Finally, discuss these important vocabulary words with students. If you think these words or other words in the section warrant more time devoted to them, there are suggestions in the introduction for other vocabulary activities (page 5).

Word	Definition	Sentence about Text
renegades (ch. 4)	people who betray an organization or a country	Hortensia tells the frightening story of when **renegades** broke into her home.
mesmerized (ch. 4)	fascinated by something and unable to look away	An excited Miguel is **mesmerized** by the locomotive as he watches it pull in.
doting (ch. 4)	very fond of someone	Observers are impressed by generous Papa, who **dotes** on the children during their train ride.
undulating (ch. 4)	moving with a smooth, wavelike motion	Esperanza watches the **undulating** land pass outside the train window.
disembarked (ch. 5)	left a vehicle	When the train stops moving, the passengers **disembark**.
stagnant (ch. 5)	having no flow or activity, often with a bad smell	The air in the train is **stagnant** with the smell of body odor.
demeanor (ch. 5)	outward behavior toward others	Mama's **demeanor** changes when she speaks to the immigration official.
untethered (ch. 5)	free; not tied down	Esperanza feels like she is floating, **untethered** and frightened.
staccato (ch. 5)	with each sound separated from the others	Esperanza's **staccato** breaths interrupt the silence.
cascade (ch. 5)	pour down quickly, like a small waterfall	Tears **cascade** down Esperanza's cheeks.

Name _____

Date _____

Understanding Vocabulary Words

Directions: The following words appear in this section of the book. Use context clues and reference materials to determine an accurate definition for each word.

Word	Definition
renegades (ch. 4)	
mesmerized (ch. 4)	
doting (ch. 4)	
undulating (ch. 4)	
disembarked (ch. 5)	
stagnant (ch. 5)	
demeanor (ch. 5)	
untethered (ch. 5)	
staccato (ch. 5)	
cascade (ch. 5)	

Name _____

Date _____

During-Reading Vocabulary Activity

Directions: As you read these chapters, record at least eight important words on the lines below. Try to find interesting, difficult, intriguing, special, or funny words. Your words can be long or short. They can be hard or easy to spell. After each word, use context clues in the text and reference materials to define the word.

- _____
- _____
- _____
- _____
- _____
- _____
- _____
- _____
- _____

Directions: Respond to these questions about the words in this section.

1. Why would people think Papa is a **doting** father?

   _____

   _____

2. What causes Mama's **demeanor** to change when she speaks to the immigration official?

   _____

   _____

Analyzing the Literature

Provided below are discussion questions you can use in small groups, with the whole class, or for written assignments. Each question is given at two levels so you can choose the right question for each group of students. Activity sheets with these questions are provided (pages 28–29) if you want students to write their responses. For each question, a few key discussion points are provided for your reference.

Story Element	■ Level 1	▲ Level 2	Key Discussion Points
Plot	How does Esperanza escape from Tío Luis?	Why does Esperanza's escape from Tío Luis have to be so secretive?	They escape to Señor Rodríguez's at night. He hides Esperanza and Mama in a secret space in the wagon and covers them with guavas. Alfonso drives the wagon to the train station. The escape must be secretive because Mama knows Tío Luis will be furious and will try to stop them from leaving.
Character	How do Esperanza and Mama react differently to the little girl on the train?	What do Mama and Esperanza's differing reactions to the little girl on the train show about their characters?	Esperanza jerks the doll away from the little girl and hides it in her valise. Mama apologizes to the girl's mother and makes the child a yarn doll. These reactions show Esperanza still thinks she is better than others because she was rich; Mama is showing kindness and realizes their lives are different now.
Setting	What things are familiar to Esperanza as they arrive in California?	What differences does Esperanza notice between the lands of Mexico and California?	The fields of crops are familiar to Esperanza, as are the roses and nearby orange grove. She notices the differing altitudes in California as they drive through the mountains and valley. In the valley, she feels dizzy because instead of the gently rolling land of Mexico, it is completely flat with repeating rows of grapes.
Character	Why does Esperanza dislike Marta?	Contrast how Marta and Isabel treat Esperanza.	Marta is rude to Esperanza, telling her Papa was bad because of his wealth and Marta's father had died fighting men like him in the revolution. She also smiles at Miguel, making Esperanza jealous, and makes fun of Esperanza for going from "princess" to "peasant." Isabel is fascinated by Esperanza, is kind to her, and sticks up for her when Marta is mean.

Name _____

Date _____

Analyzing the Literature

Directions: Think about the section you just read. Read each question and state your response with textual evidence.

1. How does Esperanza escape from Tío Luis?

_____

_____

_____

_____

2. How do Esperanza and Mama react differently to the little girl on the train?

_____

_____

_____

_____

3. What things are familiar to Esperanza as they arrive in California?

_____

_____

_____

_____

4. Why does Esperanza dislike Marta?

_____

_____

_____

_____

Name _____

Date _____

▲ Analyzing the Literature

Directions: Think about the section you just read. Read each question and state your response with textual evidence.

1. Why does Esperanza's escape from Tío Luis have to be so secretive?

    _____

    _____

    _____

    _____

2. What do Mama and Esperanza's differing reactions to the little girl on the train show about their characters?

    _____

    _____

    _____

    _____

3. What differences does Esperanza notice between the lands of Mexico and California?

    _____

    _____

    _____

    _____

4. Contrast how Marta and Isabel treat Esperanza.

    _____

    _____

    _____

Name _____

Date _____

Reader Response

Directions: Choose one of the following prompts about this section to answer. Be sure you include a topic sentence in your response, use textual evidence to support your opinion, and provide a strong conclusion that summarizes your opinion.

Writing Prompts

- **Informative/Explanatory Piece**—What problems do you think Esperanza will experience in her new life? What advice could you offer her as she gets settled in the United States?
- **Opinion/Argument Piece**—Do you think Mama and Esperanza should have stayed in Mexico or moved to the United States? Include examples to support your choice.

_____

_____

_____

_____

_____

_____

_____

_____

_____

_____

_____

_____

_____

Name _____

Date _____

Close Reading the Literature

Directions: Closely reread the section in chapter 4 when Esperanza meets Carmen, the hen lady. Begin with, "They had been on the train for four days and nights," and stop when Miguel says, "The rich take care of the rich and the poor take care of those who have less than they have." Read each question and then revisit the text to find evidence that supports your answer.

1. Since Carmen is not a main character, why does the author include her? Use the text to support your answer.

   _____

   _____

   _____

2. Give two examples from this section to show that Carmen is generous.

   _____

   _____

   _____

3. Why is Esperanza so surprised at Mama's behavior with Carmen? Use textual evidence in your answer.

   _____

   _____

   _____

4. Use Carmen's actions to illustrate what Miguel means when he says, "The rich take care of the rich and the poor take care of those who have less than they have."

   _____

   _____

   _____

Name _____

Date _____

Making Connections—Make a Yarn Doll

Directions: You can make a yarn doll just like Mama does! Follow these instructions to make a new friend for yourself or to give away.

Materials

- several yards of yarn
- 4 to 6 six-inch pieces of yarn
- a book or a DVD case
- scissors

 **Step 1a:** Loop the yarn vertically around the book/case.

 **Step 1b:** After the first loop, tie a knot (but don't cut it).

 **Step 1c:** Continue wrapping the yarn 50 to 75 times. After the last loop, tie the end to another loop and cut the yarn.

 **Step 2:** Slide a piece of yarn between the loops and the book or case. Tie it in a knot to gather all of the loops together. Slide the yarn off the book/case.

 **Step 3a:** Take 4 short pieces of yarn. Tie one where the neck should be.

 **Step 3b:** Pull 8 to 12 pieces of yarn to each side to be the arms.

 **Step 3c:** Tie pieces of yarn at the wrists and trim off the ends. Tie another short piece of yarn where the waist should be.

 **Step 4a:** For a boy doll, divide the yarn into two legs, and tie pieces of yarn at the ankles and trim the ends of the looped yarn.

 **Step 4b:** For a girl doll, the bottom can be left alone to create a skirt. The loops can be kept or trimmed to create fringe.

Name _____

Date _____

Creating with the Story Elements

Directions: Thinking about the story elements of character, setting, and plot in a novel is very important to understanding what is happening and why. Complete **one** of the following activities based on what you've read so far. Be creative and have fun!

Characters

Mama's actions and appearance seem to have changed since Papa's death. Make a Venn diagram with at least three character traits that describe her both before and after his death. The center should have at least two ways she has stayed the same.

Setting

Create a map to show the route Esperanza takes to get to the United States. Use a real map to help you find the locations of the different places.

Plot

Esperanza has to leave her home without saying good-bye to Marisol. Write a letter from Esperanza to her best friend explaining what has happened and how Esperanza feels.

Vocabulary Overview

Ten key words from this section are provided below with definitions and sentences about how the words are used in the book. Choose one of the vocabulary activity sheets (pages 35 or 36) for students to complete as they read this section. Monitor students as they work to ensure the definitions they have found are accurate and relate to the text. Finally, discuss these important vocabulary words with students. If you think these words or other words in the section warrant more time devoted to them, there are suggestions in the introduction for other vocabulary activities (page 5).

Word	Definition	Sentence about Text
bestowed (ch. 6)	presented an honor or gift	Mama wants Esperanza to be grateful for the favors **bestowed** on them.
debris (ch. 6)	scattered pieces of something broken	As a truck drives by, **debris** flies off the top.
accosting (ch. 6)	approaching someone in an aggressive, unfriendly way	The smell from the onion trucks **accosts** Esperanza's eyes and nose.
somberly (ch. 6)	in a solemn or serious way	Esperanza **somberly** thanks Miguel for teaching her to sweep.
accustomed (ch. 7)	so familiar with something that it seems normal	Hortensia says they are **accustomed** to doing things a certain way.
extravagant (ch. 7)	more than what is reasonable or appropriate	Esperanza tells Isabel about the **extravagant** parties she had in her old life.
atrocious (ch. 8)	very bad or unpleasant	Lupe's diaper smells **atrocious**.
preoccupied (ch. 8)	thinking about something so much that other things are ignored	Esperanza remembers the blanket she had been too **preoccupied** to unpack.
spore (ch. 8)	a plant cell that can make a new plant	Mama's sickness is caused by dust **spores**.
contagious (ch. 8)	able to be spread from one person to another	Josefina is relieved to learn that Mama's sickness is not **contagious**.

Name _____

Date _____

Understanding Vocabulary Words

Directions: The following words appear in this section of the book. Use context clues and reference materials to determine an accurate definition for each word.

Word	Definition
bestowed (ch. 6)	
debris (ch. 6)	
accosting (ch. 6)	
somberly (ch. 6)	
accustomed (ch. 7)	
extravagant (ch. 7)	
atrocious (ch. 8)	
preoccupied (ch. 8)	
spore (ch. 8)	
contagious (ch. 8)	

Name _____

Date _____

During-Reading Vocabulary Activity

Directions: As you read these chapters, record at least eight important words on the lines below. Try to find interesting, difficult, intriguing, special, or funny words. Your words can be long or short. They can be hard or easy to spell. After each word, use context clues in the text and reference materials to define the word.

- _____
- _____
- _____
- _____
- _____
- _____
- _____
- _____
- _____
- _____

Directions: Now, organize your words. Rewrite each of your words on a sticky note. Work as a group to create a bar graph of your words. You should stack any words that are the same on top of one another. Different words appear in different columns. Finally, discuss with a group why certain words were chosen more often than other words.

Analyzing the Literature

Provided below are discussion questions you can use in small groups, with the whole class, or for written assignments. Each question is given at two levels so you can choose the right question for each group of students. Activity sheets with these questions are provided (pages 38–39) if you want students to write their responses. For each question, a few key discussion points are provided for your reference.

Story Element	■ Level 1	▲ Level 2	Key Discussion Points
Character	How does Esperanza respond when she meets Isabel's friend, Silvia?	How does Esperanza's introduction to Isabel's friend, Silvia, show she is changing?	Esperanza's first reaction is to pull away because Silvia is very dirty. But she remembers her rudeness to the girl on the train and how it disappointed Mama. So she is kind and thinks to herself that it must be difficult to stay clean at the dusty camp. This shows she is gaining empathy and thinking of others' feelings.
Setting	What is Miguel's and Alfonso's secret surprise for Esperanza and Mama?	Why is Miguel and Alfonso's gift so important to Esperanza and Mama?	Miguel and Alfonso bring rose clippings from the garden at El Rancho de las Rosas and plant them at their new home. The roses are important because they are from Mexico and were Papa's. Mama says she knew Papa's heart would find them anywhere.
Plot	Describe Esperanza's first day taking care of the twins by herself.	How does Esperanza show she is strong during her first day alone with the twins?	Esperanza's day is very hard. She feeds the twins plums that upset their stomachs, and they have dirty diapers all afternoon; she also burns the beans for dinner. She is strong because she works through it all, cleaning the diapers, adding water to the beans, and making rice water for the twins' upset stomachs.
Plot	According to the doctor, how did Mama get Valley Fever?	Why do you think Mama has Valley Fever but no one else does?	Mama got Valley Fever during the dust storm. Dust spores got into her lungs, and they caused an infection. Mama got Valley Fever because she has not been in the valley as long as some of the others; she is weaker than the others because she has never worked.

Name _____

Date _____

Analyzing the Literature

Directions: Think about the section you just read. Read each question and state your response with textual evidence.

1. How does Esperanza respond when she meets Isabel's friend, Silvia?

_____

_____

_____

2. What is Miguel's and Alfonso's secret surprise for Esperanza and Mama?

_____

_____

_____

3. Describe Esperanza's first day taking care of the twins by herself.

_____

_____

_____

4. According to the doctor, how did Mama get Valley Fever?

_____

_____

_____

Name _____

Date _____

▲ Analyzing the Literature

Directions: Think about the section you just read. Read each question and state your response with textual evidence.

1. How does Esperanza's introduction to Isabel's friend, Silvia, show she is changing?

_____

_____

_____

_____

2. Why is Miguel's and Alfonso's gift so important to Esperanza and Mama?

_____

_____

_____

_____

3. How does Esperanza show she is strong during her first day alone with the twins?

_____

_____

_____

_____

4. Why do you think Mama has Valley Fever but no one else does?

_____

_____

_____

_____

Name _____

Date _____

Reader Response

Directions: Choose one of the following prompts about this section to answer. Be sure you include a topic sentence in your response, use textual evidence to support your opinion, and provide a strong conclusion that summarizes your opinion.

Writing Prompts

- **Opinion/Argument Piece**—Mama tells Esperanza that happiness is a choice and encourages Esperanza to choose to be happy. Do you agree with Mama? Use examples from the text to support your opinion.
- **Narrative Piece**—After the first day of work, Mama's muscles are sore and tired. Esperanza feels embarrassed and incompetent—her pride has been bruised. Write about a time when you felt like Mama or Esperanza.

_____

_____

_____

_____

_____

_____

_____

_____

_____

_____

_____

_____

Name _____

Date _____

Close Reading the Literature

Directions: Closely reread the part in chapter 7 when Esperanza is at the *jamaica*. Begin with, "The platform was lit up with big lights," and stop with, "Would they have to go back to Mexico?" Read each question and then revisit the text to find evidence that supports your answer.

1. How does Esperanza feel when she arrives at the *jamaica*? Use the text to support your answer.

   _____

   _____

   _____

   _____

2. Based on the text, why does Marta want the workers to strike?

   _____

   _____

   _____

3. Use the text to explain why the man calling back to Marta does not want to strike.

   _____

   _____

   _____

4. According to this passage, what are Josefina's feelings regarding striking?

   _____

   _____

   _____

Name _____

Date _____

Making Connections–Strike?

Directions: Do you think the workers should strike? Create a poster in the space below that shows your opinion. Your poster should include two reasons that support your belief. Make sure it is colorful and would attract attention.

Name _____

Date _____

Creating with the Story Elements

Directions: Thinking about the story elements of character, setting, and plot in a novel is very important to understanding what is happening and why. Complete **one** of the following activities based on what you've read so far. Be creative and have fun!

Characters

Divide a piece of paper into three sections. In each one, make a simple sketch showing a way Miguel has shown kindness to Esperanza. Write a description to explain each drawing.

Setting

Create an invitation for the *jamaica*. Be sure to include where and when it will happen, as well as what events will be happening.

Plot

For the first time, Esperanza has work to do in the house and in the camp. Make a detailed chore chart to help her keep track of her many responsibilities.

Vocabulary Overview

Ten key words from this section are provided below with definitions and sentences about how the words are used in the book. Choose one of the vocabulary activity sheets (pages 45 or 46) for students to complete as they read this section. Monitor students as they work to ensure the definitions they have found are accurate and relate to the text. Finally, discuss these important vocabulary words with students. If you think these words or other words in the section warrant more time devoted to them, there are suggestions in the introduction for other vocabulary activities (page 5).

Word	Definition	Sentence about Text
listless (ch. 9)	without energy or enthusiasm	Sick Mama is **listless** and weeps often.
bereft (ch. 9)	lacking something	After the harvest, the grapevines are **bereft** of their leaves.
cavernous (ch. 9)	vast, like a cave in size or shape	The wind whips through the **cavernous** shed.
repatriation (ch. 9)	the returning of a person to their place of origin	The striking workers can be rounded up and sent to Mexico because of **repatriation**.
glycerine (ch. 10)	a colorless liquid used in some medicine	Hortensia mashes avocado and adds **glycerine**.
suppleness (ch. 10)	softness; without stiffness	Esperanza loves to feel the **suppleness** of Mama's hands.
susceptible (ch. 10)	easily harmed by something	Valley Fever makes Mama's body more **susceptible** to other infections.
squalor (ch. 10)	very dirty because of poverty or neglect	Marta and her mother do not seem embarrassed by the **squalor** of their camp.
recuperation (ch. 10)	recovery from illness	Esperanza wants to avoid any threat to Mama's **recuperation**.
animated (ch. 10)	full of excitement	Miguel's face is **animated** as he talks about his job at the railroad.

Name _____

Date _____

Understanding Vocabulary Words

Directions: The following words appear in this section of the book. Use context clues and reference materials to determine an accurate definition for each word.

Word	Definition
listless (ch. 9)	
bereft (ch. 9)	
cavernous (ch. 9)	
repatriation (ch. 9)	
glycerine (ch. 10)	
suppleness (ch. 10)	
susceptible (ch. 10)	
squalor (ch. 10)	
recuperation (ch. 10)	
animated (ch. 10)	

Name _____

Date _____

During-Reading Vocabulary Activity

Directions: As you read these chapters, record at least eight important words on the lines below. Try to find interesting, difficult, intriguing, special, or funny words. Your words can be long or short. They can be hard or easy to spell. After each word, use context clues in the text and reference materials to define the word.

- _____
- _____
- _____
- _____
- _____
- _____
- _____
- _____
- _____

Directions: Respond to these questions about the words in this section.

1. Why might some people be put through **repatriation**?

   _____

   _____

2. Why is Miguel so **animated** during his conversation?

   _____

   _____

Analyzing the Literature

Provided below are discussion questions you can use in small groups, with the whole class, or for written assignments. Each question is given at two levels so you can choose the right question for each group of students. Activity sheets with these questions are provided (pages 48–49) if you want students to write their responses. For each question, a few key discussion points are provided for your reference.

Story Element	■ Level 1	▲ Level 2	Key Discussion Points
Character	Why is Mama depressed?	How is Mama's depression affecting her health?	Mama is depressed because Papa died, and she and Esperanza had to leave their home and Abuelita behind. Her depression is making it hard for her body to fight off the Valley Fever. She is strong for Esperanza at first, but she has no strength left now to get better.
Plot	Why is Esperanza upset to find out cutting potato eyes will only take three weeks?	How does Miguel convince Esperanza that cutting the potato eyes is a good idea?	She is upset because she needs to work much longer than three weeks to earn enough money to pay for Mama's hospital bills and to bring Abuelita from Mexico. Miguel tells her if she does well at this job, they will hire her to tie grapes; if she does well at that, they will hire her for asparagus. One job leads to another.
Character	Why does Esperanza give the *piñata* to the children at Marta's camp?	What does Esperanza do at Marta's camp that shows she is changing?	She gives the children the *piñata* because they have nothing, and she wants to be kind. Filling the man's hat with beans and giving away the *piñata* show that she is changing. She is not thinking only of herself and her hardships; she is sympathetic to others and wants to help.
Plot	What information does Marta share about the upcoming strike?	Why does Marta tell Esperanza about the upcoming strike?	Marta tells Esperanza that the strikers are organized and are planning to strike in a few weeks. She tells Esperanza as a gesture of friendship. Marta warns that the strikers will shut everything down, and Esperanza must be careful if she chooses to work instead of join the strikers because they will be angry.

Name _____

Date _____

■ Analyzing the Literature

Directions: Think about the section you just read. Read each question and state your response with textual evidence.

1. Why is Mama depressed?

   _____

   _____

   _____

   _____

2. Why is Esperanza upset to find out cutting potato eyes will only take three weeks?

   _____

   _____

   _____

   _____

3. Why does Esperanza give the *piñata* to the children at Marta's camp?

   _____

   _____

   _____

   _____

4. What information does Marta share about the upcoming strike?

   _____

   _____

   _____

   _____

Name _____

Date _____

▲ Analyzing the Literature

Directions: Think about the section you just read. Read each question and state your response with textual evidence.

1. How is Mama's depression affecting her health?

   _____

   _____

   _____

   _____

2. How does Miguel convince Esperanza that cutting the potato eyes is a good idea?

   _____

   _____

   _____

   _____

3. What does Esperanza do at Marta's camp that shows she is changing?

   _____

   _____

   _____

   _____

4. Why does Marta tell Esperanza about the upcoming strike?

   _____

   _____

   _____

   _____

Name _____

Date _____

Reader Response

Directions: Choose one of the following prompts about this section to answer. Be sure you include a topic sentence in your response, use textual evidence to support your opinion, and provide a strong conclusion that summarizes your opinion.

Writing Prompts

- **Informative/Explanatory Piece**—Explain why some of the workers choose to strike while others choose to continue working.
- **Narrative Piece**—What problems does Esperanza face in trying to bring Abuelita to the United States? Come up with a plan to get Abuelita back with her family.

_____

_____

_____

_____

_____

_____

_____

_____

_____

_____

_____

_____

Name _____

Date _____

Close Reading the Literature

Directions: Closely reread in chapter 10 when Esperanza goes to the market with Miguel. Begin when Esperanza says, "Miguel, why must we always drive so far," and stop with, "While Miguel drove, Esperanza began feeding in the caramels." Read each question and then revisit the text to find evidence that supports your answer.

1. Explain what Miguel means when he says, "He [Mr. Yakota] is getting rich on other people's bad manners." Use the text to support your answer.

   _____

   _____

   _____

2. According to this section, what prejudices have Miguel and Esperanza experienced or heard about?

   _____

   _____

   _____

3. How would the story be different if it occurred in another time?

   _____

   _____

   _____

4. Use examples from the text to show how Esperanza is changing from the spoiled girl who first arrived in California.

   _____

   _____

   _____

Name _____

Date _____

Making Connections–Valley Fever

Directions: Read the text below. Then, answer the questions in complete sentences.

Valley Fever is a common illness in dry desert places such as California, Arizona, and New Mexico. It is caused by a fungus that lives in the soil. A dust storm or digging in the ground can stir up the dirt, causing the fungus to be in the air. The fungus enters people's lungs as they breathe.

Many people get Valley Fever and do not even know they have it. Only about half who inhale the fungus actually get sick. People with Valley Fever feel like they have the flu. They will have a fever, a cough, and a headache but also joint pain and possibly a rash. There are medicines available, and most people make a full recovery.

1. Would a construction worker or a teacher be more likely to get Valley Fever? Why?

   _____

   _____

2. Why do you think some people who inhale the fungus get sick and others don't?

   _____

   _____

3. What could a person do to avoid getting Valley Fever?

   _____

   _____

4. What do you think would be the worst thing about having Valley Fever?

   _____

   _____

Name

Date

Creating with the Story Elements

Directions: Thinking about the story elements of character, setting, and plot in a novel is very important to understanding what is happening and why. Complete **one** of the following activities based on what you've read so far. Be creative and have fun!

Characters

Write a letter from Abuelita to Esperanza. Use information from the book and your own creative ideas to imagine what Abuelita would say.

Setting

Make a T-chart to contrast Esperanza's and Marta's camps. Include at least four differences.

Plot

Create a newspaper or magazine advertisement for Hortensia's avocado-and-glycerine hand cream.

Teacher Plans

Vocabulary Overview

Ten key words from this section are provided below with definitions and sentences about how the words are used in the book. Choose one of the vocabulary activity sheets (pages 55 or 56) for students to complete as they read this section. Monitor students as they work to ensure the definitions they have found are accurate and relate to the text. Finally, discuss these important vocabulary words with students. If you think these words or other words in the section warrant more time devoted to them, there are suggestions in the introduction for other vocabulary activities (page 5).

Word	Definition	Sentence about Text
lugs (ch. 11)	boxes or crates used for hauling fruits and vegetables	The **lugs** of asparagus have to be taken across the picket lines.
deportation (ch. 11)	the removal of a person (usually not a citizen) to leave a country	Families do not want to be separated, so they choose voluntary **deportation**.
despondent (ch. 11)	showing hopelessness and gloom	Esperanza watches the **despondent** faces of the women on the bus.
devoutly (ch. 12)	in a way that shows devotion to religion	Isabel **devoutly** prays to be made Queen of the May.
barracks (ch. 12)	a building used to house large numbers of people	The Okies will live in army **barracks** from an old military camp.
relapse (ch. 12)	the return of illness after a time of getting better	Though Mama is doing better, there is still the chance of a **relapse**.
antiseptic (ch. 12)	free of germs	The cabin is cleaned until it is almost **antiseptic** for Mama's return.
makeshift (ch. 13)	a temporary substitute for something	Mama rests on a **makeshift** lounge on the ground near the wooden table.
infuriated (ch. 13)	extremely angry	Tío Luis becomes **infuriated** when Mama and Esperanza run away.
cacophony (ch. 13)	an unpleasant mix of loud sounds	When it is finished, Esperanza's blanket forms a **cacophony** of color.

Name _____

Date _____

Understanding Vocabulary Words

Directions: The following words appear in this section of the book. Use context clues and reference materials to determine an accurate definition for each word.

Word	Definition
lugs (ch. 11)	
deportation (ch. 11)	
despondent (ch. 11)	
devoutly (ch. 12)	
barracks (ch. 12)	
relapse (ch. 12)	
antiseptic (ch. 12)	
makeshift (ch. 13)	
infuriated (ch. 13)	
cacophony (ch. 13)	

Name _____

Date _____

During-Reading Vocabulary Activity

Directions: As you read these chapters, choose five important words from the story. Then, use those five words to complete this word flow chart. On each arrow, write a vocabulary word. In the boxes between the words, explain how the words connect. An example for the words *despondent* and *deportation* has been done for you.

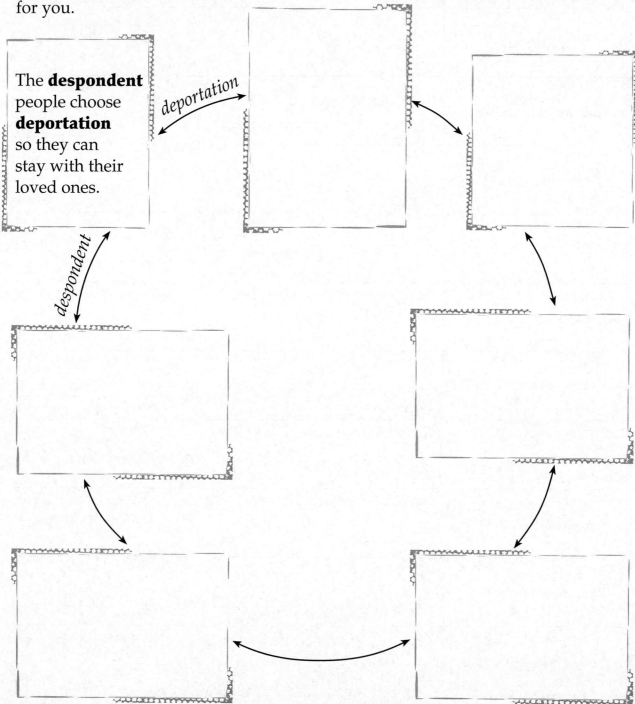

The **despondent** people choose **deportation** so they can stay with their loved ones.

deportation

despondent

Analyzing the Literature

Provided below are discussion questions you can use in small groups, with the whole class, or for written assignments. Each question is given at two levels so you can choose the right question for each group of students. Activity sheets with these questions are provided (pages 58–59) if you want students to write their responses. For each question, a few key discussion points are provided for your reference.

Story Element	■ Level 1	▲ Level 2	Key Discussion Points
Plot	How do the strikers sabotage the asparagus crates?	What do the strikers hope to accomplish by sabotaging the asparagus crates?	The strikers put snakes, rats, and broken glass in the crates to endanger the women unpacking. They do this because they are angry at the people who continue working. They want everyone to join the strike so the growers will have to listen to the strikers.
Plot	What is voluntary deportation?	Describe at least two reasons why Esperanza does not like voluntary deportation.	Voluntary deportation is when people choose to go back to their own country. In the book, immigration officials send outspoken strikers to Mexico, but their families will usually choose to go with them. Esperanza is sad to think some families might be separated, and she thinks it is unfair people would be deported for voicing their opinions.
Character	Why does everyone think Miguel took the money orders? Why does he actually take them?	Why is Abuelita's return so important?	They think he took the money orders to travel and look for railroad work. He actually takes them to go get Abuelita. Her return is important because Abuelita is the missing piece of the family. Mama and Esperanza need her, and now the United States can truly become their home because Abuelita is with them.
Character	Why does Esperanza beg Miguel to take her to the foothills?	What is the significance of Esperanza hearing the land's heartbeat?	Esperanza wants to lie on the ground and listen for the land's heartbeat. It is significant because she heard it in Mexico, her home, with Papa. When she first came to the United States, she could not hear it and felt like an outcast. Now, she has accepted her new home and can hear her land's heartbeat again.

Name _____

Date _____

Analyzing the Literature

Directions: Think about the section you just read. Read each question and state your response with textual evidence.

1. How do the strikers sabotage the asparagus crates?

   _____

   _____

   _____

   _____

2. What is voluntary deportation?

   _____

   _____

   _____

   _____

3. Why does everyone think Miguel took the money orders? Why does he actually take them?

   _____

   _____

   _____

   _____

4. Why does Esperanza beg Miguel to take her to the foothills?

   _____

   _____

   _____

   _____

Name _____

Date _____

▲ Analyzing the Literature

Directions: Think about the section you just read. Read each question and state your response with textual evidence.

1. What do the strikers hope to accomplish by sabotaging the asparagus crates?

   _____

   _____

   _____

   _____

2. Describe at least two reasons why Esperanza does not like voluntary deportation.

   _____

   _____

   _____

   _____

3. Why is Abuelita's return so important?

   _____

   _____

   _____

   _____

4. What is the significance of Esperanza hearing the land's heartbeat?

   _____

   _____

   _____

   _____

Name _____

Date _____

Reader Response

Directions: Choose one of the following prompts about this section to answer. Be sure you include a topic sentence in your response, use textual evidence to support your opinion, and provide a strong conclusion that summarizes your opinion.

Writing Prompts

- **Opinion/Argument Piece**—Abuelita says when the injured bird flew away, she knew it was a sign that whatever was wrong with Mama was better. Do you believe in signs like this? Why or why not?
- **Narrative Piece**—Now that Esperanza is surrounded by her friends and family, what do you predict will happen in her life next?

_____

_____

_____

_____

_____

_____

_____

_____

_____

_____

_____

_____

_____

_____

_____

Close Reading the Literature

Directions: Closely reread the section in chapter 12 when Esperanza and Miguel argue. Begin when Hortensia asks, "How did you get so dirty?" and stop when Miguel says, "And you still think you are a queen." Read each question and then revisit the text to find evidence that supports your answer.

1. Why does Miguel dig ditches instead of working as a mechanic?

   _____

   _____

   _____

   _____

2. Using the text, explain why Miguel feels his life in the United States is better than in Mexico.

   _____

   _____

   _____

3. Why does Esperanza feel angry and frustrated about the way Mexicans are treated? Use examples from the section to support your answer.

   _____

   _____

   _____

4. In what ways is Miguel still like a "peasant" and Esperanza still like a "queen"?

   _____

   _____

   _____

Name _____

Date _____

Making Connections—Mexican Proverbs

Directions: These two Mexican proverbs are printed at the beginning of *Esperanza Rising*. Choose one of the proverbs to write about on the lines below. Discuss the meaning of the proverb and how it relates to how Esperanza's circumstances and attitudes have changed by the end of the novel.

Aquel que hoy se cae,
se levantará mañana.

He who falls today
may rise tomorrow.

Es más rico el rico
cuando empobrece
que el pobre
cuando enriquece.

The rich person is richer
when he becomes poor,
than the poor person
when he becomes rich.

_____

_____

_____

_____

_____

_____

_____

_____

_____

_____

Name _____

Date _____

Creating with the Story Elements

Directions: Thinking about the story elements of character, setting, and plot in a novel is very important to understanding what is happening and why. Complete **one** of the following activities based on what you've read so far. Be creative and have fun!

Characters

What if Mama had not gotten sick? Make a list of at least five things that might have been different in the book. Use your list to argue that Mama's illness either helped or hurt Esperanza.

Setting

Imagine what Abuelita's life was like in Mexico without Esperanza and Mama. Write a few pages from her diary describing what was happening in Aguascalientes. Use the text and your imagination.

Plot

Create a comic strip that explains why Esperanza gave Isabel her doll from Papa. The comic should be at least five frames long and include dialogue and illustrations.

Name _____

Date _____

Post-Reading Theme Thoughts

Directions: Read each of the statements in the first column. Choose a main character from *Esperanza Rising*. Think about that character's point of view. From that character's perspective, decide if the character would agree or disagree with the statements. Record the character's opinion by marking an X in Agree or Disagree for each statement. Explain your choices in the fourth column using text evidence.

Character I Chose: _____

Statement	Agree	Disagree	Explain Your Answer
If something is unfair, people should fight for change.			
Poor people and rich people should not be friends.			
Going through a hard experience makes a person stronger.			
Starting over is too hard and not worth it.			

Name _____

Date _____

Culminating Activity: To Strike or Not to Strike

Overview: A debate is a formal discussion with opposing viewpoints between two people or groups. In *Esperanza Rising*, the decision to strike or to work has big consequences. Characters on both sides of the issue have good reasons to think they are doing the right thing.

Directions: Answer the questions below to start thinking through your opinion.

1. Why are some people striking?

   _____

   _____

2. Why are some people continuing to work?

   _____

   _____

3. If you were a character in the book, would you strike or work?

   _____

4. Use at least one example from the book to support your opinion.

   _____

   _____

   _____

5. Use at least one example from your own experience or modern life to support your opinion.

   _____

   _____

   _____

Name _____

Date _____

Culminating Activity: To Strike or Not to Strike (cont.)

Directions: Work in a small group of people who share your opinion on the topic. Fill in your group's information for each part of the debate. When you are finished, practice talking about your ideas. Be prepared for a classroom debate.

Stance
(which side of the issue you support)

_____

Opening Arguments
(list supporting arguments)

_____

_____

_____

Opposing Arguments
(list arguments the other side might make)

_____

_____

_____

Rebuttal
(list arguments to defend your ideas against opposing arguments)

_____

_____

_____

Closing
(mention your strongest supporting argument again)

_____

_____

_____

Name _____

Date _____

Comprehension Assessment

Directions: Circle the letter for the best response to each question.

1. What is the meaning of *camp* as used in the book?

    A. to sleep outside in a tent

    B. a place where a large group of people lives

    C. to voluntarily return to a person's home country

    D. a large ranch with livestock and acres of crops

2. Which detail from the book best supports your answer to question 1?

    E. "Row upon row of white wooden cabins formed long lines, connected like bunkhouses."

    F. "Some people lived in tents but others had only burlap bags stretched between poles."

    G. "Your husband, Sixto Ortega, left this house and all of its contents to you and your daughter."

    H. "Families don't want to be separated from their loved ones and usually go with them."

3. What is the main idea of the text below?

    Miguel: "The rich take care of the rich and the poor take care of those who have less than they have."

    _____

    _____

4. Choose two details that support your answer to number 3.

    A. "I am still rich, Isabel. We will only be here until Abuelita is well enough to travel."

    B. "Yet when she can barely afford it she gave your mother two hens."

    C. "She lifted the *piñata* and held it out to them [two children]. They said nothing but hurried toward her."

    D. "Her hands would never look like the hands of a wealthy woman from El Rancho de las Rosas."

Comprehension Assessment (cont.)

5. Which statement best expresses a theme of the book?

    A. Freedom of speech does not have consequences.

    B. Strikes will help people earn fair pay.

    C. Rich people do not have problems.

    D. Perseverance is important.

6. What detail from the book provides the best evidence for your answer to number 5?

    E. "Do not be afraid to start over."

    F. "We must all join together if we are all to eat!"

    G. "Something seemed very wrong about sending people away from their own 'free country' because they had spoken their minds."

    H. "He calls you *mi reina*! Will you tell me about your life as a queen?"

7. What is the purpose of these sentences from the book?: "Isabel had nothing, but she also had everything. Esperanza wanted what she had. She wanted so few worries that something as simple as a yarn doll would make her happy."

    _____

    _____

    _____

    _____

    _____

    _____

8. Which other quotation from the story serves a similar purpose?

    A. "Next week, I get to go to school, and I will learn to read."

    B. "Didn't I tell you that Papa's heart would find us wherever we go?"

    C. "Did you always get your way, and have all the dolls and fancy dresses you wanted?"

    D. "Isabel never tired of Esperanza's stories about her previous life."

Name _____

Date _____

Response to Literature: A Nation of Immigrants

Overview: The United States is a unique country because the majority of its residents are descended from immigrants. Immigrants from Mexico are the focus in *Esperanza Rising*, but people from all over the world have moved to the United States for a variety of reasons. Examples of countries with large numbers of immigrants to the United States are:

- Bosnia
- China
- India
- Ireland
- Poland
- Philippines

Directions: Select one of these immigrant groups and do research to learn more about it. When and why did many people in this group come to the United States? Where did they settle? What hardships did they face? What contributions have they made to U.S. culture? Write a researched essay that compares and contrasts your immigrant group with the immigrants in *Esperanza Rising*. Use facts and details from your research, and also cite the novel to support your thinking. In conclusion, explain your opinion about this question: *Is America really the land of opportunity?*

Your essay response to literature should follow these guidelines:

- Be at least 750 words in length.
- Cite information about your immigrant group.
- Compare/contrast your group to immigrants in *Esperanza Rising*.
- Cite at least three references from the novel.
- Provide a conclusion that summarizes your thoughts and findings.

Final essays are due on _____.

Name _____

Date _____

Response to Literature Rubric

Directions: Use this rubric to evaluate student responses.

	Exceptional Writing	**Quality Writing**	**Developing Writing**
Focus and Organization	☐ States a clear opinion and elaborates well. Engages the reader from the opening hook through the middle to the conclusion. Demonstrates clear understanding of the intended audience and purpose of the piece.	☐ Provides a clear and consistent opinion. Maintains a clear perspective and supports it through elaborating details. Makes the opinion clear in the opening hook and summarizes well in the conclusion.	☐ Provides an inconsistent point of view. Does not support the topic adequately or misses pertinent information. Lacks clarity in the beginning, middle, and conclusion.
Text Evidence	☐ Provides comprehensive and accurate support. Includes relevant and worthwhile text references.	☐ Provides limited support. Provides few supporting text references.	☐ Provides very limited support for the text. Provides no supporting text references.
Written Expression	☐ Uses descriptive and precise language with clarity and intention. Maintains a consistent voice and uses an appropriate tone that supports meaning. Uses multiple sentence types and transitions well between ideas.	☐ Uses a broad vocabulary. Maintains a consistent voice and supports a tone and feelings through language. Varies sentence length and word choices.	☐ Uses a limited and unvaried vocabulary. Provides an inconsistent or weak voice and tone. Provides little to no variation in sentence type and length.
Language Conventions	☐ Capitalizes, punctuates, and spells accurately. Demonstrates complete thoughts within sentences, with accurate subject-verb agreement. Uses paragraphs appropriately and with clear purpose.	☐ Capitalizes, punctuates, and spells accurately. Demonstrates complete thoughts within sentences and appropriate grammar. Paragraphs are properly divided and supported.	☐ Incorrectly capitalizes, punctuates, and spells. Uses fragmented or run-on sentences. Utilizes poor grammar overall. Paragraphs are poorly divided and developed.

The responses provided here are just examples of what the students may answer. Many accurate responses are possible for the questions throughout this unit.

During-Reading Vocabulary Activity—Section 1: Prologue–Chapter 3 (page 16)

1. Abuelita's **capricious** behavior includes walking barefoot in the grapes, carrying a book, and telling poems to the birds.

2. The visas must be replaced **discreetly** because no one can know Mama and Esperanza are going to leave Mexico.

Close Reading the Literature—Section 1: Prologue–Chapter 3 (page 21)

1. It will be difficult for Mama and Esperanza to stay because Tío Luis might burn down the servants' quarters if they try to stay. People will be afraid to help them because they do not want to make Tío Luis angry. If they stay in Mexico, they will have to go far away to a place where no one knows of Tío Luis.

2. Mama's plan must be kept a secret because if Tío Luis finds out, he will prevent her and Esperanza from leaving. To leave instead of marrying Tío Luis will be a great insult, and they will have to make sure they are far away by the time he finds out.

3. Abuelita is reassuring Esperanza that although things will be hard, starting over does not have to be something to fear. Abuelita had to start over as a young girl when she and her family moved from Spain to Mexico, so she is speaking to Esperanza from experience.

4. Esperanza has thoughts that she and Mama will live in a big house in California, and Alfonso, Hortensia, and Miguel will be there to take care of them. Abuelita will join them when she can and they will be away from the terrible uncle.

Making Connections—Section 1: Prologue–Chapter 3 (page 22)

- Bad luck examples may include Friday the thirteenth, breaking a mirror, walking under a ladder, or a black cat crossing your path. Good luck examples may include horseshoes, a rabbit's foot, a penny on the ground, or a four-leaf clover.

1. Esperanza pricks her finger on the thorn of a rose, which is supposed to be bad luck.

2. People believe in superstitions because they have heard them all of their lives and accept them as true. Some people believe in superstitions because they find them comforting.

3. Students should provide examples to support why they do or do not believe in superstitions.

During-Reading Vocabulary Activity—Section 2: Chapters 4–5 (page 26)

1. Papa looks like a **doting** father because Esperanza and Miguel are having fun in the fancy dining car, bouncing on the seats and ordering lunch.

2. Mama's **demeanor** changes because the official is questioning her, and she wants him to approve her entry into the United States.

Close Reading the Literature—Section 2: Chapters 4–5 (page 31)

1. Carmen's purpose is to show the other characters' reactions to her. Mama is friendly and confides in her, showing she accepts her changed position in society. Miguel admires her generosity, showing he understands what it is like to be poor. Esperanza does not think Carmen is proper, showing she is still clinging to her privileged attitude.

2. Carmen shows she is generous by offering Esperanza a sweet, giving Mama two of her six chickens, and giving food and money to the beggar woman.

3. Esperanza is surprised because this is not the way Mama would normally act. She allows Esperanza to take candy from Carmen and confides in her about Papa's death and their immigration to the United States. Mama is not acting like a wealthy woman but like the peasant she now is.

4. Miguel means that the rich do not care about the poor—the finely dressed people turn their backs on the beggar. But Carmen, who is poor and sells eggs to feed herself, gives some food to the crippled woman.

Close Reading the Literature—Section 3: Chapters 6–8 (page 41)

1. Esperanza feels out of place and lonely. Mama and Hortensia are with other women, and Esperanza wants to stay close to them instead of mingling. She sees girls who are about her age laughing and talking, and it makes her wish Marisol were there.

2. Marta feels the workers should strike because they are treated and paid unfairly. She compares the workers to the meek kittens who do not defend themselves. If all of the Mexicans work together to strike, she thinks conditions will improve for everyone.

3. The man in the crowd doesn't want to strike because he only wants to feed his family. He isn't worried about what everyone else is doing or thinking. He came to the United States to work.

4. Josefina will not strike. She says their camp is better than most and they can't afford to lose their jobs. She knows people from Oklahoma are coming for jobs, too, and if the Mexicans strike, the big farms will just hire Oklahomans.

During-Reading Vocabulary Activity—Section 4: Chapters 9–10 (page 46)

1. People might experience **repatriation** if they cause problems and their papers are found to not be in order.

2. Miguel is **animated** because he is excited to have found a job at the railroad, his lifelong dream.

Close Reading the Literature—Section 4: Chapters 9–10 (page 51)

1. Miguel means that because Mr. Yakota treats people with respect, more people come to his shop, and he can make more money. He does not call the Mexicans names like "dirty greaser," and he stocks items they want like *chiles*, *frijoles*, and *chorizo*.

2. Some of the prejudices Miguel and Esperanza are aware of are people assuming they are uneducated and only good for manual labor; segregated sections at movie theaters for Mexicans; people not wanting their children to go to school with Mexicans.

3. If the story happened in modern times, there would be less racial discrimination. There are no longer separate sections or different schools for whites, Mexicans, and African Americans. Esperanza and Miguel also would be required to go to school.

4. Esperanza shows she is changing by joking about her hardships. Her clothes are old and too big and she wears her hair in a plain braid, yet she jokes with Miguel saying, "How could anyone look at me and think I was uneducated?" She also buys the *piñata* for Mama and wants to give the candy to the nurses, showing her generosity.

Making Connections—Section 4: Chapters 9–10 (page 52)

1. Construction workers would be more likely to get Valley Fever because they work outside and dig in the dirt.

2. Some people may not get sick because their bodies are healthier and stronger.

3. A person could work indoors or wear a mask outside to avoid getting Valley Fever.

4. Student responses will vary.

Close Reading the Literature—Section 5: Chapters 11–13 (page 61)

1. Miguel digs ditches because the railroad does not want him as a mechanic. A group from Oklahoma comes and says they would work for half the money even though they had no experience. The boss tells Miguel he can dig ditches, so he does because he needs to be paid for the day.

2. Miguel's life is similar in some ways to his life in Mexico, but there is a big difference. In Mexico, he could only ever be a peasant and a second-class citizen, but in the United States, he can be more than that. He knows it is a small chance and he must work hard for it, but it can happen.

3. Esperanza is upset because people treat the Mexicans like they are dumb, dirty, and uneducated. She knows Isabel will not be Queen of the May because she is Mexican even though she has the best grades. The Okies will get a swimming pool in their camp, hot water, and indoor toilets. The Mexican camp has none of this and they can only swim in the Okies' pool the day before it gets cleaned because they are "dirty."

4. Miguel is like a peasant because he is poor, works manual labor, and cannot have the job he truly desires. Esperanza is still like a queen because she gets angry that her life is a "zigzag" like the blanket instead of in "perfect rows" like in the vineyards. She judges Miguel just as she did in Mexico by calling him a peasant and telling him he is still on the other side of the river.

Comprehension Assessment (pages 67–68)

1. B. a place where a large group of people lives

2. E. "Row upon row of white wooden cabins formed long lines, connected like bunkhouses."

3. Main idea: The poor are more generous and caring than the rich.

4. B. "Yet when she can barely afford it she gave your mother two hens." C. "She lifted the *piñata* and held it out to them [two children]. They said nothing but hurried toward her."

5. D. Perseverance is important.

6. E. "Do not be afraid to start over."

7. Esperanza realizes she is still materialistic. She wants to learn to be happy with what she has and to enjoy the small things in life.

8. A. "Next week, I get to go to school, and I will learn to read."